WATER
RESOURCES

Andrew J. Milson, Ph.D.
Content Consultant
University of Texas at Arlington

Acknowledgments

Grateful acknowledgment is given to the authors, artists, photographers, museums, publishers, and agents for permission to reprint copyrighted material. Every effort has been made to secure the appropriate permission. If any omissions have been made or if corrections are required, please contact the Publisher.

Instructional Consultant: Christopher Johnson, Evanston, Illinois

Teacher Reviewer: Linda O'Connor, Northeast Independent School District, San Antonio, Texas

Photographic Credits

Cover, Inside Front Cover, Title Page ©Hardi Budi/ National Geographic Stock. **3** (bg) ©Gary Nolton/ Getty Images. **4** (bg) ©Laurent Piechegut/Bios/ photolibrary.com. **6** (bg) ©Thomas Wolke-UNEP/Still Pictures/photolibrary.com. (cl) ©Dr. Gopal Murti/ Photo Researchers, Inc. **7** (tr) ©Joel Sartore/National Geographic Stock. **8** (bg) Mapping Specialists. **10** (bg) ©Luiz C. Marigo. **11** (bl) ©Michael Nichols/ National Geographic Stock. **12** (t) ©Rodrigo Baleia/ LatinContent/Getty Images. **15** (bg) ©Lou Dematteis/ Redux. **16** (t) ©REUTERS/China Daily China Daily Information Corp – CDIC. **17** (br) ©WENN/Newscom. **19** (bg) ©Jim Xu/Getty Images. **20** (tc) ©TEH ENG KOON/AFP/Getty Images. **22** (bg) ©Joel Sartore/ National Geographic Stock. **24** (c) NASA Goddard Space Flight Center (http://visibleearth.nasa.gov/). **25** (bg) ©Kip Evans Photography. **27** (t) ©Mark Dye/ Star Ledger/Corbis. **28** (tr) ©Fred Hirschmann/ Science Faction/Corbis. **30** (tr) ©REUTERS/China Daily China Daily Information Corp – CDIC. (br) ©Martyn F. Chillmaid/Photo Researchers, Inc. **31** (tr) ©Laurent Piechegut/Bios/photolibrary.com. (bl) ©Luiz C. Marigo. (br) ©Kip Evans Photography. (bg) ©Gary Nolton/Getty Images.

Illustrator Credits

21 (bg) Precision Graphics.

MetaMetrics® and the MetaMetrics logo and tagline are trademarks of MetaMetrics, Inc., and are registered in the United States and abroad. The trademarks and names of other companies and products mentioned herein are the property of their respective owners. Copyright © 2010 MetaMetrics, Inc. All rights reserved.

For permission to use material from this text or product, submit all requests online at www.cengage.com/permissions.

Further permissions questions can be emailed to permissionrequest@cengage.com.

Visit National Geographic Learning online at www.NGSP.com.

Visit our corporate website at www.cengage.com.

Printed in the USA.

RR Donnelley, Menasha, WI

ISBN: 978-07362-97486

14 15 16 17 18 19 20 21

10 9 8 7 6 5 4 3

WATER WO

HOW IS POLLUTION THREATENING WATER QUALITY AROUND THE WORLD?

Since water covers two-thirds of Earth's surface, no one needs to worry about wasting it, right? Wrong! About 97 percent of the world's water is saline, or salty. That leaves only 3 percent for drinking and growing crops—and 2 percent of this freshwater is frozen in polar ice or trapped in underground rock layers called **aquifers**. Yet even freshwater isn't usable if it's polluted. If we want to preserve what little water we've got, we have to clean up our act.

WHERE WATER IS FOUND ON EARTH

Oceans
96.5%

Freshwater
3.5%

Source: U.S. Geological Survey

DIRTY WATER

Pollutants are substances that make the environment and our water dirty. Drinking these substances can make people very sick. In fact, an estimated 3.3 million people die from water-related health problems every year. Most are children under the age of five.

Sometimes water pollutants come from natural sources, such as rotting plant material. Natural disasters—including earthquakes, floods, hurricanes, and tsunamis—can contaminate water sources by sweeping huge amounts of waste into them.

Animal and human waste can foul water too. Without adequate treatment, this waste can carry bacteria into water supplies. **Bacteria** are one-celled organisms that can cause diseases. In developing countries, waterborne diseases cause four-fifths of all illnesses.

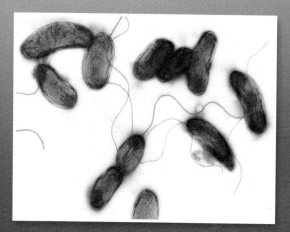

This bacteria carries cholera, a disease caused by drinking contaminated water.

If not disposed of correctly, almost everything we throw away can end up in the sea—including rusty old bicycles.

HUMAN ACTIONS

Other sources of pollution are human-made. Chemicals, including pesticides and fertilizers, are among the largest sources of pollution. Scientists say that the world's water supplies contain more than a million different chemicals.

Pollution also comes from burning **fossil fuels**, such as coal and oil. These energy sources are formed by the fossilized remains of plants and animals that have been buried in the earth for millions of years. When coal and oil are burned for energy, gases are released that mix with water vapor in the air. This vapor condenses and falls to Earth as acid rain, which pollutes lakes, streams, and

It may take years to undo the damage to wildlife caused by the 2010 Gulf of Mexico oil spill.

rivers. In addition, accidents that occur when companies drill for oil can damage our waters. An oil spill at sea can contaminate sea life, beaches, and birds.

Developing countries that do not have clean water and adequate sanitation suffer high rates of disease, poverty, and hunger. Many countries are determined to fight water pollution. They've found ways to treat dirty water and clean up their polluted waterways.

In the following pages, you will read about two places—South America's Amazon River and China's Lake Tai—that have had serious water pollution problems. People in both places are trying to clean up their waterways. Their efforts show that we can do something about water pollution.

Explore the Issue

1. **Summarize** What are some of the sources of water pollution?

2. **Analyze Cause and Effect** What impact does water pollution have on humans?

Industrial Water

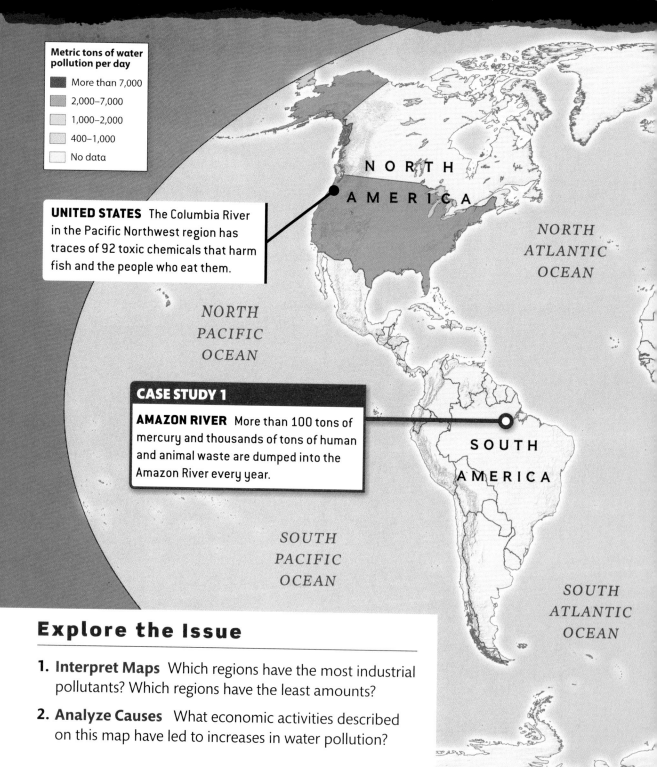

Metric tons of water pollution per day

- More than 7,000
- 2,000–2,000
- 1,000–2,000
- 400–1,000
- No data

UNITED STATES The Columbia River in the Pacific Northwest region has traces of 92 toxic chemicals that harm fish and the people who eat them.

NORTH AMERICA

NORTH ATLANTIC OCEAN

NORTH PACIFIC OCEAN

CASE STUDY 1

AMAZON RIVER More than 100 tons of mercury and thousands of tons of human and animal waste are dumped into the Amazon River every year.

SOUTH AMERICA

SOUTH PACIFIC OCEAN

SOUTH ATLANTIC OCEAN

Explore the Issue

1. **Interpret Maps** Which regions have the most industrial pollutants? Which regions have the least amounts?

2. **Analyze Causes** What economic activities described on this map have led to increases in water pollution?

Pollution

Study the map below to learn about the industrial pollutants that are damaging water throughout the world.

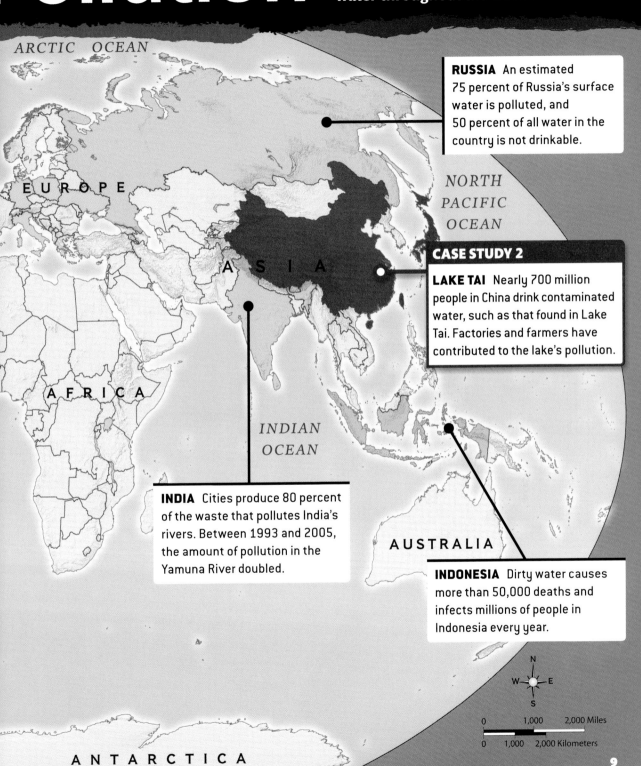

ARCTIC OCEAN

RUSSIA An estimated 75 percent of Russia's surface water is polluted, and 50 percent of all water in the country is not drinkable.

EUROPE

NORTH PACIFIC OCEAN

ASIA

CASE STUDY 2

LAKE TAI Nearly 700 million people in China drink contaminated water, such as that found in Lake Tai. Factories and farmers have contributed to the lake's pollution.

AFRICA

INDIAN OCEAN

INDIA Cities produce 80 percent of the waste that pollutes India's rivers. Between 1993 and 2005, the amount of pollution in the Yamuna River doubled.

AUSTRALIA

INDONESIA Dirty water causes more than 50,000 deaths and infects millions of people in Indonesia every year.

N
W E
S

| 0 | 1,000 | 2,000 Miles |

| 0 | 1,000 | 2,000 Kilometers |

ANTARCTICA

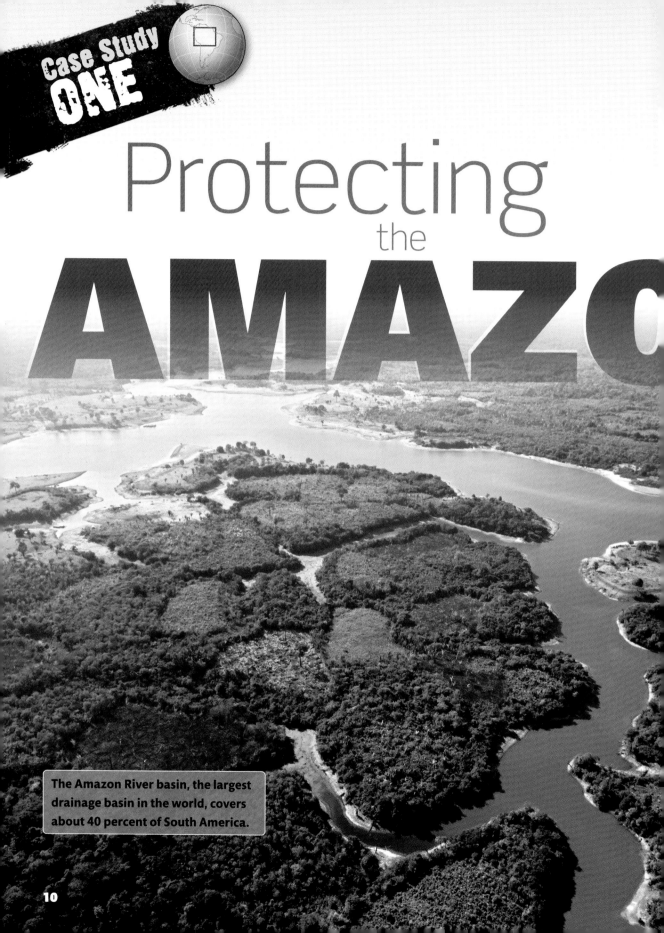

Protecting
the
AMAZC

The Amazon River basin, the largest
drainage basin in the world, covers
about 40 percent of South America.

A MIGHTY RIVER

The Amazon is the second longest river in the world. It starts high in the Andes Mountains, flows across Peru and Brazil, and empties into the Atlantic Ocean.

The Amazon River **basin** consists of the whole area drained by the river. The basin is enormous—more than 2.7 million square miles. It is also one of Earth's most diverse ecosystems. An **ecosystem** is a community of living organisms and their natural environment.

The Amazon River basin is home to approximately 10 million people and more than 30,000 plant species and 1,300 kinds of birds. It is also the world's pharmacy. Many medicines come from rare plants that grow only in the Amazon basin. We rely on the Amazon's vast rain forest to pump oxygen into the atmosphere—and freshen the planet's air.

AMAZON GOLD RUSH

Yet for years, the Amazon has faced several threats. For example, did you know that you can mine rivers for gold? Deep in the Amazon rain forest, miners scoop dirt from the riverbed. Then they treat the dirt with **mercury**, a highly toxic element that attaches to tiny gold flakes in the mud and makes the gold easier to collect.

After using the mercury, some of the mining companies dump it into the Amazon. The poisonous elements in mercury do not dissolve in water. When mercury flows downstream, it leaves destruction in its path.

Fish are the first to die. Tons of dead fish have washed up onto the banks of the Amazon. Then the animals that eat these fish are poisoned. Finally, people who drink polluted water or eat the poisoned fish and animals become sick. The mercury attacks people's brains and nervous systems and can injure unborn children.

This once fertile bank along the Amazon has been devastated by gold mining.

WATER NOT FIT TO DRINK

The global demand for energy also causes pollution woes for the Amazon. South America is rich in oil and natural gas. Companies drilling for these resources, though, have left behind huge messes. In Peru and Ecuador, oil spills and dumped toxic waste have contaminated the Amazon.

This pollution has threatened the native Achuar (osh–wahr) people of Peru, who depend on the river for food and water. One Achuar leader said, "The water in our streams is not fit to drink, and we can no longer eat the fish in our rivers or the animals in our forests."

Tribal leaders claim that the pollution has sickened native peoples in these areas. Those people who have been exposed report more illnesses, tumors, and skin ailments. The Achuar say these medical problems come from drinking water and eating fish from sites contaminated by industry.

In September 2010, a drought left this boat stranded in the Amazon basin and uncovered piles of trash and debris.

HOW CAN GROWING FOOD CAUSE POLLUTION?

Oil drilling isn't the only practice that causes pollution in the Amazon. Growing food in the Amazon rain forest has also harmed the region. The rain forest covers about 1.4 billion acres of the Amazon basin, but it was once even bigger. Over the last 40 years, nearly 20 percent of the rain forest was destroyed to make way for farms and ranches.

In Brazil, the increased number of farms and ranches has enriched the country's economy. Today Brazil is one of the world's leading suppliers of soybeans and beef products. Yet success has come at a price. Soybeans need a steady diet of fertilizers and pesticides to thrive. In addition, the cattle produce a great deal of waste. Many of these pollutants end up in the Amazon River.

HOW MUCH WATER DOES IT TAKE?

TYPE OF FOOD	AMOUNT OF FOOD PRODUCED	AMOUNT OF WATER REQUIRED
milk	1 gallon	1,000 gallons
rice	1 pound	1,978 gallons
beef	1 pound	9,304 gallons

Source: National Geographic Society

BATTLE TO SAVE A FRAGILE GIANT

In the 1960s and 1970s, people began to understand that the Amazon River and rain forest were being harmed. They started to see the effects of water pollution on all forms of life. They also began to appreciate how vast and vulnerable the Amazon's ecosystem is.

As a result, indigenous people, or those who live in the Amazon basin, started fighting to preserve the rain forest and battle polluters and illegal loggers. In the last 45 years more than 300 local environmental organizations have formed in the Amazon River basin.

Today protecting the Amazon River is a global concern. The United Nations is involved as are many other multinational organizations. Why? Scientists now think that conditions around the Amazon may affect climate as far away as Europe. It is in everyone's best interest to keep this region healthy.

TURNING THE TIDE

The fight to protect the Amazon is far from over, but progress is being made. Fewer trees are being cut down now as countries punish illegal loggers and set limits on how land is used. At the same time, stricter mining laws now forbid the use of mercury in mining.

Meanwhile, the Achuar people have united to demand a stop to oil drilling in their region. They insist that the oil companies clean up the Amazon and its **tributaries**, which are the smaller rivers and streams that flow into a larger river.

Because of the Achuar people and others, parts of the Amazon are cleaner today than many other rivers. This shows that when people band together to clean up waterways, they can make their own lives better. What's more, they can have an impact far beyond their own communities.

Explore the Issue

1. **Analyze Problems** What activities have polluted the water of the Amazon River?

2. **Analyze Solutions** What steps have South Americans taken to fight water pollution? How successful have their efforts been?

Achuar men travel by canoe along the Amazon. The river has long been a source of food and water for the Achuar.

China's POWER

THE COSTS OF INDUSTRIALIZATION

Since the 1980s, China's economy has grown quickly. New industries have developed, and new factories have been built. By 2010, the country had become the largest exporter of goods and the second largest economy in the world.

China's booming economy has brought prosperity to many of its people, but it has also had some negative effects. The new industries have led to increased levels of pollution. In fact, today about three out of every four of the country's lakes are polluted. Of course, China, like other emerging economies, is in the early stages of industrialization. As its economy develops, the country will undoubtedly take steps to deal with its pollution problem. In fact, it has already begun to do so. Meanwhile, however, pollution is harming China's rivers and lakes.

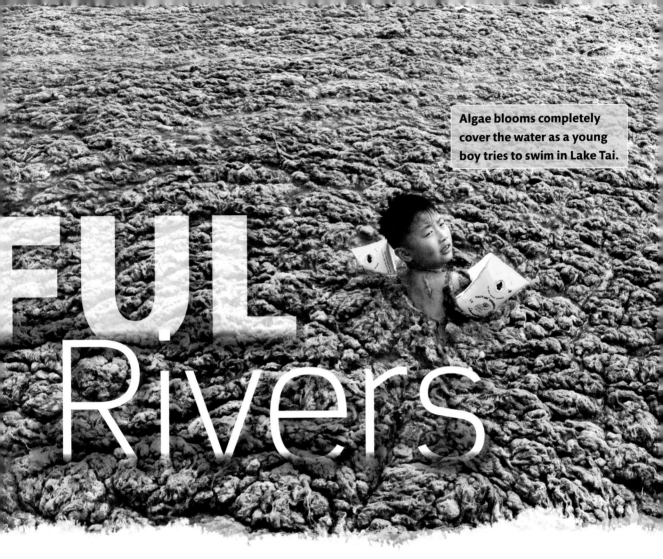

FUL Rivers

Algae blooms completely cover the water as a young boy tries to swim in Lake Tai.

THE DECLINE OF LAKE TAI

Factories cause some of China's water pollution problems. Many dump chemical waste into nearby waterways. As a result, harmful chemicals such as arsenic and ammonia show up in lakes and rivers.

Pollution from factories and other causes resulted in the decline of Lake Tai, China's third-largest body of freshwater. In the 1950s, the Chinese built dams near the lake to control floods. However, the dams also reduced the lake's ability to clean and protect itself from harmful pollutants. When factories dumped massive amounts of chemicals into the lake, the pollution caused **algae**, or plantlike organisms, to grow. So much algae grew that it sucked the oxygen out of the lake and suffocated its plants and fish.

Algae stains this man's hands green and makes the water in Lake Tai undrinkable for local residents.

DAMAGED DRINKING WATER

Although Chinese officials knew their country had a pollution problem, for years they only studied the effects of industrial pollution on bodies of water. Then in 2007, they began to record the discharge from farms and landfills. Based on this information, Chinese officials realized that water pollution levels were more than twice as high as they had originally thought.

Some of this pollution is caused when cities dump raw **sewage**, or human and animal waste, into lakes and streams. People who drink this water are taking in disease-causing bacteria.

Sewage has also damaged China's coastline. In 2006, about 8.3 billion tons of raw sewage were dumped off the southern coast of the country. Oil pipeline leaks and spills further pollute China's coastline and seas.

THE CONSEQUENCES OF WATER POLLUTION

All of this pollution takes a terrible toll on human health. In China, millions of people have become sick from drinking dirty water. Experts estimate that water pollution kills nearly 100,000 Chinese people each year. Scientists believe that more people may suffer from stomach and liver cancer in China than anywhere else in the world. They put at least part of the blame on water pollution. Furthermore, water pollution is thought to cause thousands of birth defects.

In addition to health concerns, nearly half of China's 660 major cities face water shortages as a result of the country's polluted waterways. Because so many of China's lakes, rivers, and streams are polluted, more than 300 million Chinese people lack water that is clean enough to use for irrigating crops, drinking, or washing clothes. Instead these people are turning to underground water supplies. However, they risk using up those too. The World Bank has warned China that water pollution could have "catastrophic consequences for future generations."

CHINA'S WATER POLLUTION BY THE NUMBERS

278
Number of cities in China without water-treatment facilities

450
Number of people in southern China who were poisoned by arsenic in the drinking water in 2008

22 thousand
Tons of red dye water that a T-shirt factory dumped into a river every day

700 million
Number of Chinese who drink polluted water every day

Sources: British Broadcasting Corporation, 2008; *Wall Street Journal*, 2007

People wash their clothes in a highly polluted river in the city of Guiyu (GWAY-yoo), China. Countries around the world send used computers and other electronic waste to Guiyu for disposal. The waste causes severe pollution problems for the city.

SPEAKING OUT ABOUT POLLUTION

In 2006, the Chinese government acknowledged that the country has a big water pollution problem. Officials recognized the problem after people began speaking out. For more than a decade, Wu Lihong snapped photographs of factories dumping chemicals into Lake Tai. He mailed the photos to the government. Eventually, officials cracked down on the factories, and pollution eased in Lake Tai.

These bottles are filled with contaminated water from Lake Tai.

Today more Chinese citizens are concerned about pollution. They are talking to the media and leading protests. In response, China has spent billions on new wastewater treatment plants. The plants clean the water that is taken from lakes and rivers in a process similar to the one shown at right. In 2007, 126 treatment plants dotted the upper stretches of the Chang Jiang. By the end of 2009, the river had 240 treatment plants.

A HEALTHY ENVIRONMENT

For right now, the Chinese people face a difficult choice. On the one hand, they want to do a better job protecting the environment. On the other hand, the Chinese want to keep growing their economy. Chinese citizens can afford more cars, homes, and electronic devices than ever before. Yet continued growth depends on expanding industry, which often has meant worsening pollution. Can the Chinese build business while cleaning up their water? Can they have both health and wealth? Time will tell.

Explore the Issue

1. **Analyze Causes** What are some of the different sources of water pollution in China?

2. **Analyze Effects** What has been the impact of water pollution on the Chinese people?

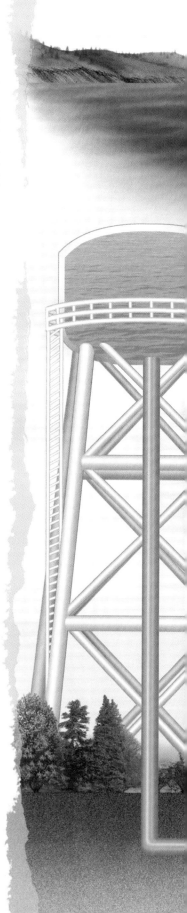

WATER PURIFICATION PROCESS

Water treatment plants in China help clean up the water in the Chang Jiang. Follow the water through the purification process.

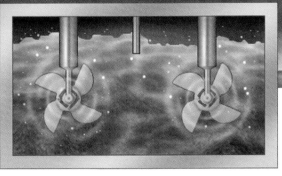

❶ COAGULATION
Safe chemicals are added to water from lakes or rivers to attract dirt particles.

❷ SEDIMENTATION
The heavy particles settle to the bottom of the basins.

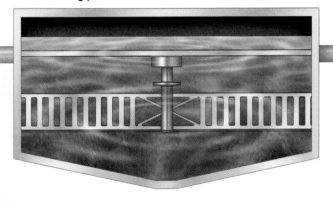

❸ FILTRATION
Clear water passes through filters that remove even smaller particles of dirt. A small amount of disinfectant is then added to kill remaining bacteria.

❹ STORAGE
Water flows to tanks where disinfection is completed and is then piped to homes.

Source: U.S. Environmental Protection Agency

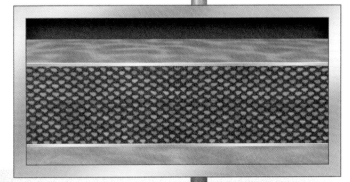

Marine
Protected Areas
& Water
Pollution

Smoke rises from the surface of
the Gulf of Mexico as cleanup
crews burn oil spilled in 2010.

GULF OIL SPILL

In November 2010, scientists diving deep in the Gulf of Mexico saw something disturbing on the ocean floor. Massive coral formations were dead or dying and covered with a strange, thick black substance.

The scientists weren't sure what the black substance was, but they had a theory—oil from the huge spill caused when the Deepwater Horizon oil drilling platform exploded in April 2010. It was another example of the pollution caused by humans. In this case, human carelessness damaged one of the world's richest ecosystems.

For all their power, oceans are fragile. They give us food, oxygen, and predictable weather. In return we give them trash, carbon dioxide, and agricultural runoff. That's not a very fair trade, and now the oceans are showing the effects. In some of these waters, fish are disappearing, and all marine life is suffering.

S.O.S. = SAVE OUR SEAS

We need to protect our seas, and National Geographic is answering the call. The organization is now teaming with scientists concerned about ocean health. Two of those scientists are Sylvia Earle and Enric Sala, Explorers-in-Residence at National Geographic. Earle and Sala are working with government agencies around the world to help establish marine protected areas, or MPAs. **Marine protected areas** are regions in or near oceans where human activity is limited in order to preserve marine life.

Some MPAs are focused on restoring our oceans' fish populations. Others nurture a fragile ecosystem or preserve a historical site. Some scientists are also using MPAs to research and document how healthy seas function in order to learn how to preserve them.

Marine protected areas are one way people can help fight the effects of pollution, overfishing, and habitat destruction. Overfishing occurs when fish are caught faster than they can be replaced by the marine population in a body of water. Of course, more efforts are needed, but MPAs give environmental groups and governments a good place to start.

RESTORING OUR OCEANS' HEALTH

Both Earle and Sala are passionate about preserving our oceans. Earle is an **oceanographer**, or scientist who studies oceans and marine life. In 2010, the Sylvia Earle Alliance teamed with the National Geographic Society and the Waitt Foundation to found Mission Blue. Mission Blue is a global partnership dedicated to restoring the oceans' health and productivity and establishing more MPAs.

Sala is a marine ecologist who grew up exploring the sea off Spain's coast. Today he heads the Pristine Seas project. The project works to find, study, and preserve healthy, undisturbed ocean sites. Along with establishing MPAs in the Mediterranean, Sala hopes to use this knowledge to help restore damaged marine environments.

Our planet's health starts—or ends—with the state of the oceans' health. You can join National Geographic in making a positive difference. First, learn all you can about the issues. Read up on water pollution, overfishing, and climate change. Then get involved. The activity on the next two pages can help you get started and inspire your own passion for preserving our water.

HOPE SPOTS The dots on this map represent the MPAs—Hope Spots— that Earle has helped establish through Mission Blue.

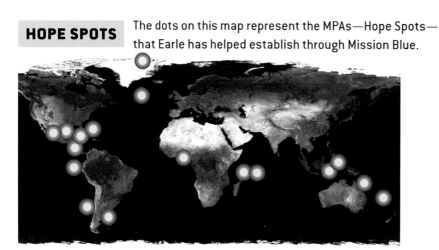

Explore the Issue

1. **Analyze Causes** What are three causes of pollution in the ocean?

2. **Explain** Why are Sylvia Earle and Enric Sala helping to establish marine protected areas?

"With every
breath we take,
every drop of
water we drink,
we're connected
to the ocean."
—Sylvia Earle

National Geographic Explorer-
in-Residence Sylvia Earle
explores the sea off the coast of
Honduras in Central America.

What Can I DO?

Rescue a River

—and report your results

You don't have to be a marine scientist to fight for our water sources. You just have to care—and get involved. One way to help is to identify a polluted river, lake, pond, or stream in your community and clean it up. With a little bit of work, you can make a big difference.

IDENTIFY

- Find out about the quality of the water sources in your community.

- Talk to experts at your local museum, university, or local water department to identify a body of water that needs help.

- Ask what steps you can take to clean up the water or improve it in other ways.

ORGANIZE

- Advertise in your school paper or place posters in your neighborhood to recruit volunteers.

- Gather the supplies you'll need to clean up: gloves, garbage bags, shovels, and water-testing kits.

- Identify an appropriate place to dispose of the garbage.

Volunteers pick up trash along the Rahway River in New Jersey.

DOCUMENT

- Take before-and-after photos of the site and perform before-and-after water tests to measure the results of your work. Have an adult help you take the tests and dispose of the water.

- List the pollutants you find and the strategies you use to deal with them.

- Videotape and interview the volunteers about their experiences.

SHARE

- Use your photos and videos to create a multimedia presentation of your cleanup effort and show it to your class.

- Describe your efforts—and the difference you made—in an article for your school or community paper.

- Inspire others to take up the battle by sharing your story and your ideas for reclaiming water sources in a talk at your local library.

Research &
WRITE
Explanatory

Write an
Informative Article

Lake Erie, which is one of the Great Lakes, was in terrible shape during the 1960s. But in an amazing turnaround, much of Lake Erie is clean today, and fish and vegetation are thriving. How did people bring Lake Erie back to life? *That* is the topic you will research and write about.

RESEARCH

Use the Internet, books, and articles to research and answer the following questions:

- What condition was Lake Erie in during the 1960s?
- How had the lake become so polluted?
- How was the lake cleaned up?

As you conduct your research, be sure to take notes in your own words and keep a list of the sources you use.

DRAFT

Review your notes and then write a first draft.

- Introduce your topic—the pollution of Lake Erie—in the first paragraph. Organize your ideas using strategies such as cause and effect and chronological order.
- Develop your topic in the second paragraph with relevant facts from credible sources to explain how people cleaned up Lake Erie. Use transitions and precise language and maintain a formal style.
- Provide a concluding section in the third paragraph to explain what the effects of the cleanup of Lake Erie have been.

REVISE & EDIT

Read your first draft to make sure that it gives solid information about the cleanup of Lake Erie.

- Does your first paragraph introduce your topic?
- Does the second paragraph develop your topic and clearly explain how people cleaned up Lake Erie?
- Have you described the effects of the cleanup effort in your conclusion in the third paragraph?

Revise the article to make sure you have covered all the bases. Then check your paper for errors in spelling and punctuation. Are names spelled correctly? Are quotations accurate? Be sure you have the information in a logical order.

PUBLISH & PRESENT

Now you are ready to publish and present your article. Add any images or graphs that will help illustrate or support your ideas. Then print out the article or write a clean copy by hand. Post the article in your classroom to share with the class.

Visual GLOSSARY

algae

mercury

algae *n.*, plantlike organisms

aquifer *n.*, an underground rock layer containing water

bacteria *n.*, one-celled organisms that can cause diseases

basin *n.*, the area drained by a river

ecosystem *n.*, a community of living organisms and their natural environment

fossil fuel *n.*, an energy source such as coal, oil, and natural gas, formed by the fossilized remains of plants and animals

marine protected area *n.*, a region in or near an ocean where human activity is limited in order to preserve marine life

mercury *n.*, a highly toxic silver-white element that is liquid at room temperature

oceanographer *n.*, a scientist who studies oceans and marine life

pollutant *n.*, a substance that makes the environment and water dirty

sewage *n.*, human and animal waste

tributary *n.*, a smaller river or stream that flows into a larger river

pollutant

oceanographer

basin

INDEX

SKILLS